GW01398784

Original title:
A Sweet Christmas Delight

Copyright © 2024 Creative Arts Management OÜ

Author: Lorenzo Barrett
ISBN HARDBACK: 978-9916-90-878-5
ISBN PAPERBACK: 978-9916-90-879-2

Nibbles of Joy and Candied Memories

Tiny treats on silver trays,
Gingerbread men start to sway.
Marshmallow fluff spills everywhere,
Who knew snacking could cause a scare?

Lollipops that dance and spin,
Chocolate rivers, let's dive in!
Frosting fights and sugar rush,
In this chaos, we all hush.

The Essence of Joyful Gatherings

Cousins giggle, uncles munch,
A fruitcake flops, but we laugh a bunch.
Potato chips in grandmas' dip,
Who knew gravy could also slip?

Tinsel tangles in our hair,
Candy canes everywhere, beware!
A holiday toast with fizzy cheer,
We cheer for snacks, oh bring them near!

Bows of Love and Cookies Galore

Ribbons wrapped around each box,
Cookies shaped like silly fox.
Sneaky bites when no one's here,
Caution to crumbs, oh dear, oh dear!

Brownies stacked like little hills,
Sugar high gives us all thrills.
Sprinkles flying through the air,
Who did this? We just don't care!

Sweet Serenades on Winter's Breath

Melting snowflakes, hot cocoa sip,
Fudge falls off the holiday trip.
Laughter echoes, what a night,
Winter's breath, a sweet delight.

Socks that match? Quite a shock,
Under the tree, a dancing flock.
Candied oranges, a surprising find,
The best moments, one of a kind!

Frosty Mornings and Honeyed Hearts

Frosty mornings greet our eyes,
With snowflakes dancing from the skies.
My nose is red, my cheeks are too,
I swear this hat is just for you.

Hot cocoa spills upon my coat,
I think this mug's now set afloat.
A marshmallow snowman, round and sweet,
Just another Christmas silly treat.

Sugar Crystals on Evergreen

The trees are decked in sparkly cheer,
Looks like they've found the candy sphere.
My dog just jumped for a hanging treat,
Now he's tangled in the garland's seat.

Sugar crystals, oh what a sight,
Did Santa trip? I think he might!
Falling branches with a gentle snap,
Who knew that joy could make you clap!

Carols of Candy Canes

We sing our songs with jingle and glee,
But why's the cat stuck up the tree?
A candy cane slipped from my grip,
Lands right on grandma's holiday trip.

Laughter echoes as we all cheer,
Who knew the fun would cost a beer?
With every laugh a joy we find,
Oops—watch out for that snowball blind!

Delights Wrapped in Flannel

Wrapped in flannel, cozy and warm,
Hot pie awaits, a delectable charm.
Grandpa's snoring, a festive sound,
As cookies vanish from the ground.

The roast is burning, what a mess,
Did someone order the holiday stress?
With every giggle, hearts take flight,
Let's create chaos, on this merry night!

Starry Skies and Cinnamon Wishes

Under twinkling stars so bright,
Santa's hat won't fit just right.
Reindeer dance on candy canes,
Laughing loud, ignoring rains.

Pumpkin pie left out to chill,
Elves find it, enjoy the thrill.
Holiday socks with holes galore,
Search for gifts, can't find the door.

Tinsel and Treats under the Mistletoe

Tinsel tangled in the tree,
Cats think it's their fancy spree.
Mistletoe hangs, I slip and fall,
Pudding stains on the wall.

Grandpa's jokes, a comic feat,
He claims he can't feel his feet.
Cookies hidden, but who can tell?
I'll wrap my cat, she knows it well.

Cocoa Kisses by the Firelight

Cocoa spills and frothy mess,
Marshmallows float, what a guess!
Firelight dances, shadows play,
A snowman's hat, blown far away.

Sipping slowly, what a dream,
Whipped cream clouds make me scream.
A fruitcake joke, it brings a laugh,
I'll slice it once, but not the half!

Snowflakes and Sweets in the Moonlight

Snowflakes fall with little grace,
Stick to noses, make a face.
Frosty is now wearing shades,
On the ice, I shift and fade.

Sweets abound, my belly aches,
Got lost in the candy flakes.
Moonlight sparkles, shadows creep,
I'll be up, I cannot sleep.

Kindred Spirits and Sweet Delights

In the kitchen, chaos reigns,
Flour on faces, laughter remains.
Cookies shaped like tiny reindeer,
Burnt, but nobody minds, my dear.

Sugar sprinkles, a colorful mess,
Frosting wars? Oh, what a test!
Gingerbread folks, with gummy hats,
Dancing around, just like crazy cats.

Radiant Lights and Sticky Sweets

Twinkling bulbs that blink and shine,
Caught in lights, we lose our lines.
Candy canes that stick like glue,
On my shoe, oh what a view!

The dog steals treats, oh what a sight,
Chasing him under the twinkling light.
Sticky fingers, laughter loud,
In this mayhem, we're all quite proud.

Whipped Cream Wonders of the Night

Spilling cream in a bubbly swirl,
A spoon in chaos, oh what a whirl!
Toppings tumble, a frothy shock,
This dessert's now a fluffy rock!

Squirting cream until I squeal,
Sundae mountain, agree it's real!
Friends all giggle, our faces smeared,
In this sticky fun, we persevere.

Charmed with Chocolate Dreams

Chocolate rivers flow so sweet,
Oops! Fell in, what a treat!
Bellyaches from bites so bold,
But we laugh, for memories unfold.

Truffles tossed like snowflakes fly,
Cocoa dust, oh my oh my!
Covered in chocolate, what a mess,
In each bite, sheer happiness.

Tis the Season for Tantalizing Treats

Gingerbread men in a dance,
Chasing after the sugar chance.
Frosting rivers, sprinkles rain,
Sugar highs, a joyful strain.

Cookies hiding in a jar,
Sneaky snacks that go too far.
Milk mustache on each sweet face,
Holiday cheer in every place.

Chocolate snowflakes woefully melt,
On the kids' tongues, pure joy felt.
Marshmallow snowmen, puffed up proud,
Giggles burst from the happy crowd.

Eggnog spills and laughter loud,
A cookie crash, the floor's a shroud.
Santa's belly jiggling delight,
Culinary chaos, what a sight!

Sweetness in the Stillness of Night

In the silence, cookie crumbs fall,
A midnight snack, the best of all.
With each nibble, starlight gleams,
Dreams of cream and sugary dreams.

The pie-wielding cat likens the moon,
Sneaking bites to a merry tune.
Milk dribbles down under the glow,
A funny sight, we all know.

Spritz cookies whisper soft and sweet,
While candy canes make their retreat.
Laughter echoes, stockings sway,
In our hearts, the joy will stay.

Baking fails lead to giggly fights,
Flour storms in festive nights.
Still we gather, smiles so bright,
For moments shared, pure delight.

Letters to Santa and Biscotti Dreams

On parchment plush, we write with glee,
Dear Santa, won't you bring us spree?
Biscotti dipped in cocoa's bliss,
Each bite wrapped in a savory kiss.

Socks stuffed with treats, what a plan,
Chocolate blocks, a holiday span.
The cat gets cozy on the stack,
As we dream of goodies, all on track.

Marzipan haikus, such crafty art,
The joke's on us, we all eat smart.
Oh, the chaos in fuzzy jammies,
Sugar highs powering our Grammys.

Wrapping presents, paper everywhere,
The tape's gone wild, it caught my hair.
With sprinkles scattered throughout the room,
It's a sweet frenzy to banish gloom.

Enchanted Nights with Sprinkles of Joy

Under twinkling lights, we roam,
Searching for sweets that call us home.
Popcorn chains and candy sleds,
Laughter spins like noodle threads.

Whipped cream mountains piled so high,
Marshmallows float like clouds in the sky.
Chasing whispers, the gingerbread tales,
While brownie bears avoid the fails.

The dog steals a sweet from the plate,
Kitchen heists that we anticipate.
Pudding puddles that slip and slide,
In every giggle, the joy can't hide.

Frosting fights in the midnight glow,
Turning desserts into a show.
With sprinkles flying, what a blast,
Enchanting nights, we hope they last!

Miracles Wrapped in Ribbons

Cats in hats, on trees they climb,
Chasing baubles, oh what a crime!
Grandma's cookies, they all disappear,
Milk spills everywhere, the end is near.

Uncle Joe's sweater, a sight to see,
Knitted with love, but smells like brie!
Laughter echoes in the snowy air,
As we untangle the lights with care.

Sparkling Moments of Seasonal Bliss.

Jingle bells ringing, but wait, what's that?
Rover's dancing, wearing a hat!
Snowflakes land on noses with glee,
As we sip cocoa while piled on three.

Dad's new dance moves could use a break,
Twisting and turning, we're all awake!
A snowman's grin, made from an old mop,
That's what you get, when you can't shop!

Joyful Echoes of Frosted Nights

Pies on the table, and cream on the floor,
Kids racing past, they come back for more!
Lights flashing wildly, a disco delight,
We dance through the hall, like it's midnight.

Mom's secret sauce, we'll surely regret,
Tummies are rumbling, it's not over yet!
The dog snags a present, oh what a prank,
We laugh 'til we cry, and then we sank.

Winter Whispers and Sugarplum Dreams

Reindeer are hiding, behind the tree,
Whispers of mischief, who could it be?
Gifts wrapped in papers, with bows that are bright,
But where's the candy? It took a flight!

A snowball fight breaks out with a splash,
Who knew a snowman could take such a bash?
Mittens are lost, and laughter spills wide,
As we tumble inside for a warm, cozy ride.

Marshmallow Whirls and Fireside Thrills

In the kitchen, chaos reigns,
Flour clouds and sugar trains,
Laughter rises, some dough flies,
As we bake, the time just flies.

Hot cocoa spills, oh what a sight,
Sipping quickly, then a fight,
Whipped cream dances, goes astray,
A marshmallow lands on Uncle Jay!

Stockings hung with little care,
What's that smell? Oh, do beware!
Cookies stuck to every pan,
We're still laughing; yes, we can!

By the fireside, tales are spun,
Each goofy joke adds to the fun,
Even the dog joins in the cheer,
Wagging his tail and stealing beer!

Trinkets of Joy Amidst Winter's Glow

Hats and mittens, mismatched too,
Oh dear Santa, what did you do?
A reindeer lost his nose today,
He swears he left it by the sleigh!

Twinkling lights above the street,
Flickering bulbs are such a treat,
Grandma's knitting, still a sight,
That sweater? It's five sizes tight!

Snowmen smile, yet one fell down,
His carrot nose rolled right to town,
Sleds flying through the crisp white flakes,
And jumps turn into huge snow shakes!

Chasing cats around the tree,
Oh what fun, oh woe is me!
The tinsel tangled, what a plight,
Still, joy shines so warm and bright!

Marzipan Dreams and Holiday Whimsy

Marzipan dreams, oh what a treat,
Funny shapes and flavors sweet,
A gummy bear leads a parade,
As grandma frowns, her plans are laid!

Nuts and spices fill the air,
Cookies shaped with love and care,
But one by one, they disappear,
As cousin Joe draws ever near!

The table groans with pies and cakes,
Each slice leads to silly shakes,
A pie fight feels like pure delight,
Oh watch the whipped cream take flight!

Chilling tales of holiday cheer,
Friends and family gather near,
With silly hats and goofy smiles,
We sit together for a while!

Mulled Magic and Kindred Spirits

Mulled magic in a mug held tight,
Sipping slowly, what a sight,
Frosty windows, cheeks so red,
Uncle Fred just spills instead!

Yule logs crackle, laughter too,
Silly stories break right through,
Gifts wrapped poorly make us squeal,
What's in that box? Just a wheel!

With friends around, the games begin,
A masquerade, who let the dog in?
Chasing shadows, spinning 'round,
Shrieks of joy, the best sound found!

In cozy corners, spirits soar,
With every giggle, we want more,
These happy moments, so sublime,
Embrace the fun, let's freeze time!

Candied Joys in Silent Nights

Marshmallow snowflakes fall from the sky,
Hoping to float by the nose of a pie.
Chocolates jump high, with a wink and a cheer,
While licorice sticks pull a prank on the deer.

Sugarplum giggles tickle the air,
Laughter erupts from a twinkle-toed bear.
Frosted trees dance in a cotton-candy swirl,
As jellybeans tumble and give us a whirl.

Gingerbread Kisses and Cocoa

Gingerbread men skip with frosting galore,
One lost a shoe, can you believe it's a chore?
Hot cocoa bubbles with marshmallows afloat,
While mug-hugging kittens are busy to gloat.

A spoonful sings sweetly, in harmony grand,
With peppermint twirls that just can't quite stand.
Sprinkles collide like confetti in flight,
As cookies conspire to party all night.

Celestial Treats of December

Candy canes twist like dance partners do,
Jelly-filled orbs pop and giggle with you.
Fudge fairies scatter their sparkly light,
As gumdrop galaxies sparkle so bright.

Cereal snowflakes crunch underfoot,
While tinsel from trees wears grape-flavored soot.
Marzipan comets zoom through the sky,
Chasing each other with a whimsical sigh.

The Warmth of Cinnamon Tales

Cinnamon sticks tell stories of cheer,
While nutmeg gives hugs that are tasty, my dear.
Baking rhymes round in a buttery bowl,
And sugar sprinkles dance with a goal.

An apron's the cape of a hero in disguise,
Flour clouds rise, oh what a surprise!
Baking disasters cause giggles galore,
With spritz cookies rolling right out the front door!

The Magic of Marzipan Mornings

In the kitchen, there's a scare,
A marzipan mouse squeaks everywhere.
With sugar coats and almond hats,
It steals the cookies—how about that?

The pancakes dance and syrup spins,
A breakfast feast with silly grins.
I swear the toast just winked at me,
This morning's fun, oh what glee!

Jam jars giggle, fruit flies twirl,
Cereal boxes start to swirl.
A spoon does somersaults in cheer,
Marzipan dreams, the best time of year!

Festive Fables in Frost

Once upon a time, you see,
A snowman drank hot chocolate tea.
He laughed so hard, his carrot flew,
Right onto my hat—oh what a skew!

The reindeer danced in funny prose,
While Santa's sleigh got stuck, who knows?
With snowballs tossed and giggles loud,
They formed a jolly, frozen crowd!

Icicles hung like disco lights,
Sleigh bells jingled in snowy nights.
Join the fun, don't miss the show,
Through frosty fables, let laughter flow!

Lullabies of Lollipops

Beneath the stars, lollipops sway,
A candy chorus sings and plays.
They spin and twirl in a frothy romance,
With gumdrops stepping in a wobbly dance.

Chocolate bunnies hop on by,
With jelly beans that seem to fly.
They tumble down, what a mess,
A stick of peppermint—oh, I confess!

Sweet dreams wrapped in sugar coats,
This sugary tale, it sure evokes.
Join in the fun, it's a sugary bliss,
In the land of lollies, you can't miss!

Flavors of Cheer in the Chill

The snowflakes sprinkle ginger snaps,
While cozy naps turn into claps.
With cheerful mugs of cocoa tight,
Marshmallows float like stars at night.

A pie takes flight, into the sky,
With whipped cream clouds that giggle high.
They bake up cheer, it's quite surreal,
In flavors that warm, oh what a meal!

With cookies winking from their plate,
Don't be too late, it's your fate!
Taste the joy that fills the air,
With every bite, forget your care!

Maple and Mirth beneath the Stars

Maple syrup on my head,
Feeling silly, see me spread.
Pancakes flying through the air,
I swear, it's a maple fair!

Mirthful laughter, friends all near,
Maple scent, it's time to cheer!
Sticky fingers, giggles loud,
Dancing, jumping, in a crowd!

Stars above are twinkling bright,
A pancake battle? What a sight!
We flip and flop, our syrup glows,
A sticky mess, but everyone knows!

Laughter echoes in the night,
Maple dreams take joyous flight.
With every bite we share our glee,
Beneath the stars, we're wild and free!

Snowy Encounters of Delightful Taste

Snowflakes tumble, what a show,
Hot cocoa's here, let's drink it slow.
Marshmallows swim a sugary dance,
One big gulp, oh what a chance!

Snowmen giggle, hats askew,
Carrots flying, how about you?
In the snowy chaos, laughter swirls,
Chasing friends, and snowball whirls!

Cookies hidden in a snowbank,
Who could resist? Let's give thanks!
But wait, what's that? A crumbly trail,
Leading to the gingerbread jail!

With every bite, a giggle grows,
Chilly cheeks, and frosty toes.
A laughter spree, a taste parade,
In snowy fun, our worries fade!

Cupcake Wishes and Holiday Hugs

Cupcakes piled, a mountain high,
Frosting clouds that touch the sky.
Sprinkles flying, oh what a sight,
Take a bite, it's pure delight!

Holiday hugs from everyone,
Squeezed so tight, oh, what fun!
With every hug, a cupcake flies,
In this chaos, joy never dies!

Pine tree smells, the oven warms,
Sugar cookies, a myriad of forms.
We frost and sprinkle, make a mess,
Caught in batter—oh yes, no less!

Wishes whispered on frosting peaks,
Giggly grins, and wobbly cheeks.
We cheer and laugh with cupcake cheer,
Gather 'round, the season's here!

Starlit Strolls with Treats in Tow

Starlit strolls on winter nights,
Treats in tow, oh what delights!
Candy canes and chocolate bars,
Navigating through sweetly bizarre!

Elves on scooters, racing by,
"Catch us if you can!" they cry.
With every step, a laugh erupts,
In the night, our fun corrupts!

Gumdrops scatter like mini stars,
Silly antics, no need for cars.
Bouncing laughter, joy's parade,
In this playground, friendships made!

As we share our favorite snack,
The sweetest taste along the track.
Under stars, our hearts align,
In these moments, all is fine!

Dance of Cookies and Mirthful Memories

Cookies twirl in sugar grooves,
Frosting smiles, it really approves.
Sprinkles bounce like tiny towns,
They wear the best of silly crowns.

Milk moustaches on our grins,
Gingerbread men do backflips, wins!
We laugh as crumbs leap in delight,
A cookie jar's dizzying height!

Marshmallow fluff clouds our heads,
We dream of candy-coated beds.
With every bite, a giggle soars,
Joyful crunches, who needs chores?

Cinnamon stars in a swirling race,
Whipped cream wins the silly chase.
Together we munch, the fun won't stop,
Cookie dance parties—let's pop!

Festive Feasts and Cheerful Raindrops

Pudding plops with a jolly thud,
As turkey floats down like a big mud.
Laughter echoes 'round the table,
While eager taste buds start to fable.

Mashed potatoes join the joyful cheer,
In gravy rivers, they disappear.
Veggies march in with goofy glee,
Football fruitcake, oh let it be!

Candied yams in a daring race,
Fluffy rolls try to take their place.
Each bite brings loud and silly sounds,
Giggling 'til the last crumb bounds!

Pies stack high, like a sugar mount,
Whipped cream splats, much fun to count.
Festive feasts fill our playful hearts,
Once done, we dance, let's restart!

Snow-dusted Dreams and Candy Crushes

Snowflakes tumble, oh what a sight,
Frosty noses in the soft moonlight.
Candy canes sprout on snowy trees,
While the laughter drifts on the breeze.

Sleds whiz past in a giggling rush,
With marshmallows plopped in a fluffy hush.
Hot cocoa spills from our goofy cups,
As we tumble over like playful pups.

Frosty friends made from mounds of fluff,
With carrot noses, they strut and puff.
We toss snowballs, but they sprout legs,
Running off, we cherish those pegs!

Gumdrop dreams in a colorful swirl,
Snowmen's antics make laughter whirl.
With candy crushes and sweet sleigh rides,
Joy is the magic that never hides!

Magic Moments with Nutmeg Sprinkles

A whisk in hand, a swirl of cheer,
The spice of life, we hold so dear.
With cookies baked, the laughter flies,
While flour dust becomes the skies.

In every bite, a giggle hides,
As taste buds dance on merry rides.
With nutmeg dreams and icing swirls,
We're happy bakers, boys and girls.

Fireside Tales and Holiday Snacks

Gather 'round with treats galore,
S'mores and popcorn, we all adore.
With stories shared, the sparks ignite,
As shadows dance in cozy light.

Toasty toes and laughter loud,
In silly hats, we feel so proud.
The snacks abound, oh what a sight,
As sweet and salty ignites the night.

A Symphony of Carols and Sweet Surprises

Jingle bells and giggles play,
With candy canes, we sing all day.
The melodies lift, their spirits high,
As gummy bears begin to fly.

With harmonies sweet, we spin around,
In every note, a treat is found.
Our joyful chorus fills the air,
With laughter bursting everywhere.

Cherries and Cheer in the Frosty Air

Outside it's cold, but we're so bright,
With cherry pies, we take our bite.
Hot chocolate flows, and mugs are raised,
In winter's chill, we are amazed.

The frosty air can't freeze our fun,
As snowballs fly and we all run.
With fruits so red and spirits light,
We dance together, hearts delight.

Frosted Promise of Delightful Days

Snowmen grinning, hats askew,
With carrot noses, what to do?
Mittens mismatched, too much cheer,
Sipping cocoa, oops! It's near!

Elves in chaos, toys in flight,
Candy canes stuck in the light.
Pine trees battling for the spot,
Sparkling tinsel, oh what a lot!

Jingle bells echo with a laugh,
Santa's sleigh, a wobbly craft!
Reindeer prancing, slipping 'round,
Hilarity in every sound!

Cookies crumbling, crumbs galore,
Whiskers twitching, there's still more!
Chasing shadows of the night,
Merry chaos, what a sight!

Festive Hearts and Gingerbread Memories

Gingerbread men dancing with glee,
Frosting smiles as wide as the sea.
Sprinkles flying, oh what a scene,
Flour on noses, so sugary clean!

Grandma's recipe, a lovely mess,
Mice in aprons, what a success!
Mixing batter, giggles abound,
Sugar highs spinning 'round and 'round!

Socks overstuffed with goodies galore,
Stamps on letters, yet more to store.
Each little present, a surprise so bright,
Under the tree, well tucked for the night!

Wrapping paper, a hard-to-beat fight,
Scissors tangled in horrific plight.
Laughter erupts, it's all in fun,
Celebrations—till it's done!

Candles that Dance in December's Embrace

Candles flicker, a wiggly dance,
Wax dripping down, take a chance.
Shadows prancing across the wall,
Giving everyone a laugh, that's all!

Mittens tangled on the chair,
Someone's snoring, unaware.
Cupcakes with faces, were they intended?
Flavors confused, but nobody's offended!

Chains of popcorn, oh what fun,
Tangled and knotted, a race to run.
Laughter echoes in the hall,
'Tis the season for it all!

Silly hats and reindeer games,
Puns aplenty, all the same.
Festive cheer, what's here to stay?
Merry madness—hooray, hooray!

Twinkling Lights and Sugar Dreams

Twinkling lights strung on the eaves,
Raccoons peeking, what a tease!
In the chaos, we find our way,
Singing loudly, come what may!

Sugar cookies stacked way too high,
Eating one, oh my, oh my!
Chilly breeze sends giggles strong,
Laughter erupts, what could go wrong?

Socks filled up and hung with care,
Mice in pajamas, unaware!
Dancing around, tinsel ablaze,
Warm hearts amidst the winter haze!

Chasing snowflakes, caught in awe,
All around hear the joy and claw!
Festive caps on everyone's head,
Spreading cheer, enough said!

Whispers of Winter Sugar

In the pantry, cookies dance,
Sugar sprinkles make them prance.
Elves in snowflakes flip and twirl,
Gingerbread men in a sugar swirl.

Hot cocoa's laughter fills the air,
Whipped cream mustache, a festive flare.
Marshmallow snowballs, all around,
Sippin' cocoa, joy is found.

Snowflakes whisper secrets sweet,
As stockings wait for a tasty treat.
Peppermint swirls with a wink,
Chomping candy canes, what do you think?

Frosted cookies, oh what a sight,
Nibble and giggle, pure delight.
Winter's magic, a goofy flair,
Laughing together without a care.

Frosted Wishes on Pine

Pinecones glisten with frosty cheer,
Twinkling lights invite us near.
Baking pies with a quirky grin,
Dancing flour, it's a win!

Socks hung up with jelly beans,
Mismatched slippers, silly scenes.
One-eyed snowman, can't find his hat,
Laughter echoes, imagine that!

Winter winds carry giggles bright,
Snowball fights under the moonlight.
Carols sung in a lopsided tune,
Lemon drops beneath the spoon.

Frosted cookies stacked, oh dear,
Who knew that eating would bring such cheer?
Christmas spirit mixed with fun,
Got to share, but can we run?

Twinkling Stars in Sugarplums

Sugarplum fairies dance in glee,
Bouncing like bunnies, wild and free.
Candied dreams float in the air,
While giggles spill everywhere.

Twinkling lights and silly hats,
Raising cups with clinks and chats.
Silly Santa, led by a kite,
Who'd have thought he'd take to flight!

Cookies crumble beneath our weight,
Eating them all? That's our fate!
Sprinkles rain like winter cheer,
Around the table, friends draw near.

Chocolate rivers, marshmallow lakes,
Frosty fun, that's what it takes.
With every bite, we raised our cheer,
Here's to laughter, and holiday beer!

Marshmallow Dreams by the Fire

By the fire, stories arise,
Toasted marshmallows, sweet surprise.
S'mores created with gooey grace,
Chocolates melting in a warm embrace.

Friends sporting hats, all askew,
Cocoa spills, a lively crew.
Singing songs from a mismatched sheet,
Winter nights can't be beat!

Pine-scented giggles filled the room,
While paper snowflakes began to bloom.
A dance-off with reindeer on the floor,
Falling over, who could ask for more?

At the end of the sparkly spree,
When sleepyheads call, "pick me!"
Dreams of sweetness fill the night,
A snuggly hug, till morning light.

Festive Cheer and a Dash of Sugar

Jingle bells are ringing loud,
With cookies shaped like Santa proud.
The snowman's nose is just a bean,
That little kid, he starts to scream!

Carols sung by a cat, oh dear,
As everyone piles up on cheer.
Gingerbread men run from the tray,
They dance around, they laugh and play.

Hot cocoa spills on mom's new dress,
While Uncle Joe just can't suppress,
His love for pie with extra cream,
A holiday, it seems, a dream!

And when the lights begin to twinkle,
That turkey dance could make you wrinkle.
So raise a glass of fizz tonight,
To laughter shared, and all that's bright!

Flurries of Laughter on Winter Paths

On snowy streets where snowballs fly,
A rogue one hits my dad nearby.
He slips and giggles with delight,
'Tis the season to be polite!

In mittens lost, a search begins,
The dog runs off with all our sins.
He's wearing gifts, bright bows galore,
Around the tree, he plays and soars.

The sledding hill, a sight to see,
With kids who tumble endlessly.
Grandpa's fall, a graceful twist,
A flurry of laughter we can't resist.

And cocoa drips from pastel mugs,
While Auntie knits with cozy hugs.
These moments shared, a sparkling glow,
In winter's chill, we steal the show!

Chilling Joys of Spiced Delights

The oven's warm, it beckons treats,
With cinnamon and nutmeg feats.
But oops, I dropped a tray of pies,
Now they resemble Christmas flies!

The cat is sneaking 'round the edge,
While Grandma sits upon a ledge.
"Don't feed the dog!" she laughs aloud,
He's eyed the cookies, full of clouds.

My brother's prank with sticky glue,
Leaves us all in quite the stew.
The cookies look like Christmas art,
But taste like coal, oh where's my heart?

Yet every bite, a tale to share,
With laughter filling up the air.
These chilling joys, a funny game,
In spice we found our little fame!

The Yuletide Confectionery Tales

Here comes the cake with layers wide,
A mountain tall, we can't abide.
Slicing through, it gives a fight,
Who knew it weighed a ton, alright?

The candy canes, oh what a trick,
Get stuck in hair and makes us sick.
Our stockings full, but what a mess,
With bubble wrap, we must confess.

Then carols sung by off-key choirs,
While popcorn strands catch fire in spires.
A ginger snap both fierce and light,
Turns into chaos by the night.

Yet as we laugh and munch away,
These tales of sugar, joy, and play.
With festive cheer we'll fill our wells,
In Yuletide dreams and cookie spells!

Evergreen Hugs and Spiced Laughter

The tree it sways, a little askew,
With ornaments hung by a cat named Lou.
Tinsel tangles in his furry hair,
As he treats it like just a jungle fair.

Gifts piled high with ribbons untied,
Grandpa gets stuck in the reindeer slide.
Cookies crumble, a floury mess,
Who knew baking could be such a test?

Singing loudly, we've lost the key,
Mom's off pitch, but it's all so free.
Carols echo from the fridge's hum,
As we dance to tunes from a playful drum.

Mistletoe's hanging, we just can't see,
Uncle Joe's the unwitting decree.
A peck on the cheek, then a sprightly spin,
Oh, what a sight, let the laughter begin!

Wrapped in Love and Cinnamon Whirls

The cookies are soft but a tad too brown,
Dad's chef ambitions are widely renowned.
We toss sprinkles like confetti in glee,
But somehow, they land all over me!

Hot cocoa froths with marshmallows gone wild,
Sister's concoction, terribly compiled.
A sip brings laughter, a dash brings cheer,
But sip it slowly, or else it's a smear!

The lights are twinkling with a sassy flair,
Grandma's dance moves could spark a fair stare.
She twirls and twirls, quite the sight indeed,
Until she bumps into an unsolicited feed.

With cinnamon swirls and hugs that unfold,
We share all the tales our memories hold.
Laughter bubbles softly, like soda in flight,
Next year, let's hope it's a little more right!

Warmth of Yuletide's Embrace

A snowman wobbles, his buttons askew,
Two eyes from rocks say, 'How do you do?'
The scarf has slipped, and he's frowning now,
Time for a snowball; better watch out, wow!

The fire crackles like old friends in chat,
While the cat plots schemes, oh where's she at?
Mittens and hats in a tangled array,
We giggle and fuss as we slip away.

Pine-scented air and laughter combined,
As Aunt May's fruitcake has everyone blind.
One bite and your face reveals all the dread,
But we smile politely, just nodding instead.

Under the mistletoe, kisses abound,
That awkward uncle, oh what a clown!
With warmth that we share, you can't help but cheer,
This funny old season, we hold it so dear.

Cocoa Cheers and Marzipan Wishes

The cocoa flows with a splash and a swirl,
While Marzipan monsters begin to unfurl.
They dance on the table, wiggle their feet,
A wobbly treat that can't be beat.

The fireplace roars, and the children all sing,
But one little brother just yanked on a string.
Now ornaments crash with an audible *thud*,
And we all learn laughter is a sweet kind of blood.

Stockings are stuffed, but where's the good stuff?
A sock full of lumps, oh, this is just rough!
But who needs the presents when joy fills the air?
With giggles and hugs, there's love everywhere.

So let's raise our cups filled with sugary dreams,
Toast all our blunders, or so it just seems.
Happy and silly, we gather round tight,
To cherish the chaos of this festive night.

Warm Hearth and Candied Cheer

Gather 'round the glowing fire,
Uncle Joe's got socks to hire!
Grandma's baking quite a spread,
With fruitcake that we'll all dread.

Kids sneak bites of gingerbread,
While the cat gets crumbs instead.
A partridge on the mantel sits,
But all he does is throw some fits.

Mom's been mixing drinks galore,
Last year's punch pegs us to the floor.
Laughter fills this crowded space,
As we all attempt a race.

The eggnog spills, oh what a sight,
We toast and laugh into the night.
Such joy in every goofy cheer,
Here's to memories year by year!

Boughs of Holly and Tasty Delights

In the kitchen, flour flies,
While Aunt Sue tries to bake pie.
Just don't ask to taste the mix,
Unless you like some chocolate tricks!

Boughs of holly hang with pride,
While Timmy takes the cookie ride.
Frosting is his main delight,
He dons a beard that's oh-so-white!

Silly hats with bells go jingle,
As doggo joins in with a mingle.
Nuts and treats stacked high and wide,
Who knew a squirrel could act so spry?

Chasing crumbs across the floor,
Wondering if there'll be more.
Between the laughter and the bites,
This feast will end in silly nights!

A Chorus of Cookies and Hot Chocolate Wishes

Hot cocoa flows, it's dripping sweet,
But someone's spilled, oh what a feat!
Marshmallows leap onto the floor,
Making it hard to open the door.

A chorus sings, off-key and loud,
Mom just laughs, she's so proud.
Cookies burn, the smoke alarm,
Yet somehow, it still has charm.

We pose for photos in delight,
With goofy grins, what a sight!
But, cousin Fred just can't hold still,
In his reindeer suit, he fits the bill!

Then snowflakes start to dance outside,
But we've all got our goofy pride.
In this mix of joy and cheer,
We're thankful for each funny year!

Sweeter Than Ever Under the Tree

Presents piled under the tree,
Will someone pick my socks? Oh gee!
The cats are playing with the bows,
While Aunt Jean snags the last of those.

Lights twinkle hide-and-seek all night,
As we share stories, laughter, and fright.
With every joke and silly tale,
We all know that we can't fail.

It's the season of merry and fun,
Even the parrot joined the run!
Screaming 'Merry!' at the top of his lungs,
As we all hum those classic songs.

Underneath this twinkling glow,
Sweets abound, but they move so slow!
From candy canes to bites of pie,
We'll feast together, oh my, oh my!

Stars and Silverbells

The stars are twinkling, quite the show,
Silverbells ringing, oh what a glow.
Santa slipped on ice, what a sight,
The reindeer just chuckled, took flight.

Mistletoe hanging, a trap for the shy,
A kiss from Aunt Edna? Oh my, oh my!
Gifts piled high, like a game of Jenga,
Watch it all fall, "Oops! Where's the media?"

Cookies laid out, but where did they go?
Rats in the kitchen? No, just my bro!
He's sneaking some snacks while we sing loud,
Pretending it's him, but we'll blame the crowd.

Eggnog spills from a wobbly hand,
This festive chaos is just so grand.
Let's dance round the tree, just don't break a light,
It's a jingle, a jangle, a laugh-filled night!

Peppermint Hugs in Winterfields

Snowflakes flutter like feathers in flight,
We roll up a snowman, oh what a sight!
A carrot for a nose, and buttons so bright,
Then he tips over, what a funny plight!

Peppermint sticks, oh they look so sweet,
But watch out for Grandma, she's quick on her feet.
She lunges for sweets, but trips on her shoe,
In winterfields, laughter's the best glue.

Snowball fights start, but I'm quite the aim,
I throw one at Uncle, he's not quite the same.
"Who threw that?" he cries, with a face like a plum,
Just don't tell him… or else we'll all be done!

Chill in the air, it tickles the nose,
While we deck the halls with ribbons and bows.
As we sip our cocoa and snicker away,
This winter field fun makes a perfect display!

Tinsel and Tarts under the Tree

Tinsel is shimmering, hanging with flair,
But wait, what's that? A cat with a stare!
She leaps for the baubles, in quite a thrill,
It's a holiday hazard, a near epic spill!

Tarts on the table, oh, what a feast,
But someone's sneaky, like a hungry beast.
Fingers in frosting and faces so round,
Who knew our party would come to this sound?

Christmas songs jingle, out of tune cheer,
Dad's off-key crooning, and laughter we hear.
With tinsel in hair, my brother's a sight,
We're all having fun in this wild, merry plight.

Laughter erupts like the pop of a cracker,
And Grandma, the dancer, she sure is a whacker!
Under the tree, these memories will stay,
Tinsel and tarts—what a whimsical play!

Joyous Echoes of Yuletide

Echoes of laughter fill up the room,
Mom's making stew—oh, that smell makes me zoom!
Uncle Joe's stories, they bring such a cheer,
Until he tells one, for the fifty-ninth year.

Jingle bells jangle, but who's got the keys?
Cousin Timmy's hiding, "It's not me, please!"
But when he finds them, oh what a race,
As he zooms through the house, we're all red in the face!

Later we gather, around the warm fire,
To roast some marshmallows, our own goofy choir.
With giggles and pokes, we tell silly tales,
While sparks rise up, and giggles prevail.

In this quirky season, where joy is the tune,
The echoes of laughter, like stars, make us swoon.
With every odd moment, this memory's gold,
These joyous echoes are treasures untold!

Cookie Crumbles and Frosty Breezes

The cookies danced, oh what a sight,
Frosting battles, a sugary fight.
Sprinkles flew, as we took a bite,
Laughter echoed, pure delight.

The pans were piled, a mountain high,
A gingerbread man waved goodbye.
We thought we'd bake, but whoops, oh my!
Flour storms made us all cry.

With crumbs and giggles all around,
A cupcake landed, oh what a sound!
We threw some frosting, oh what a round,
In this sweet chaos, joy is found.

The milk was spilled, like a snowy blast,
With each sweet disaster, we had a blast.
Next year we'll bake—let's hope it lasts,
But who will clean up? That's a different cast!

Sweetness on the Winter Breeze

Santa slipped on a chocolate bar,
Chimney smoke reached up afar.
Cookies left for him and his car,
But who would guess, it's a cookie bazaar!

The carolers sang with frosty breath,
While kittens danced, oh what a mess!
They snagged the treats, no time to rest,
In this festive chaos, we're truly blessed.

Pinecones dropped like fruity bombs,
Holiday cheer with giggly qualms.
With every sip of spiced-up balms,
Dry snowflakes tumbled, defying psalms.

Oh the ribbons! They tangled tight,
A candy cane fence made our night.
With cheeky smiles and pure delight,
We danced 'til dawn, all feeling light!

Evergreen Embrace of Dulcet Notes

Under the tree, a squirrel popped,
With acorns—was that a new drop?
He stole my cake, quick as a hop,
While I just stood, mouth agape, a flop!

Jingle bells clanged, as I tripped and fell,
In a tangle of lights, oh what the hell!
With candy canes, we rang the bell,
To call the fun, all is well!

We tried some songs—out of tune,
The dog howled loud, beneath the moon.
The reindeer pranced in a festive swoon,
While baked goods vanished, quite a monsoon!

Gingerbread houses had a riot,
A marshmallow fight? Oh, let's not be quiet!
With laughter and joy, let's share the diet,
In this sweet winter, we found our defiant!

Holiday Harmony in Sugarcoated Smiles

The stockings hung, but what a sight,
Filled with candy, oh what delight!
The cat jumped up, oh what a fright,
As we opened treats—oh what a bite!

Tinsel tangled like a giant mess,
While we tried to clean in a powdery dress.
My uncle slipped with a sugar kiss,
As laughter erupted, oh what bliss!

We sipped hot cocoa, marshmallows afloat,
Dripped all over that candid quote.
The laughter rang from throat to throat,
In this silly game, we happily gloat.

Oh what a night with friends so dear,
Jokes and jests filled the atmosphere.
With a burst of joy and festive cheer,
We welcome the season, all gathered near!

Wishes Floating on Winter Winds

Frosty flakes dance with glee,
As snowmen grin mischievously.
Hot cocoa's swirling in my cup,
Just try to keep this smile up!

Gifts wrapped tight, but where's the fun?
My cat's the one who's on the run!
She pounces on the ribbons bright,
Oh dear, what a festive sight!

Children laughing, voices ring,
What joy a snowball fight can bring!
But watch your back and dodge the throws,
Or wear a hat full of white snows!

So here's a wish on winter's breeze,
May laughter come with greatest ease.
With merry tricks and playful cheer,
Let's celebrate this time of year!

Jingle Bell Serenade of Joy

Jingle bells jangle, what a tune,
As squirrels dance beneath the moon.
The tree's aglow, lights flashing bright,
But where's my gift? It's out of sight!

A reindeer snoozes on the lawn,
While kids all sing till dusk is gone.
Elves are giggling, sneaking treats,
I hope they don't take all my sweets!

Neighbors bake with flour galore,
Oh no! I think they've baked me more!
Cookies shaped like frosty hats,
I guess I'll share with the neighborhood cats!

So jingle all the way, I say,
Let's have fun this special day.
A laugh or two will warm the night,
Come join the jolly, pure delight!

Stars, Spice, and Joyful Flurries

Under twinkling stars we glide,
With gingerbread in tow, we ride!
Snowflakes spin in tasty swirls,
Like my cousin's wild, hilarious hurls!

Cinnamon lingers in the air,
While Grandma's wig wiggles with flair.
She's baking pies, but don't you fret,
She'll bake the one we won't forget!

The fireplace crackles, tales unfold,
Of Santa's sleigh, the magic bold.
But wait, what's that? The cat's on the shelf,
Knocking down ornaments, full of himself!

So let's toast to the jolly night,
With laughter echoing pure delight.
May our hearts be light and bright,
In this funny holiday light!

Laughter in the Snowy Silence

The world is wrapped in frosty white,
But in our home, there's pure delight!
A snowball sneaks in through the door,
Watch out! My brother's set to score!

We build a fort, it's quite the sight,
Made of snow that's fluffy and light.
Then moose and penguins come to play,
But only in our dreams, I say!

Sledding down the hilariously steep,
We tumble over, laugh and leap.
Snowmen sport a hat askew,
And sprinkle glitter, oh if they knew!

So in this snowy, stilling hush,
Let giggles rise and spirits rush.
For in the silence, we'll remember,
The laughter sparkles like a ember!

Milton Keynes UK
Ingram Content Group UK Ltd.
UKHW021837301124
451618UK00007BA/246

9 789916 908785